And Then I Got Fired:

One Transqueer's Reflections on Grief, Unemployment & Inappropriate Jokes About Death

By J Mase III

Cover Photo by: Ajamu X

ISBN #: 978-0-359-49472-9

I hope this
book speaks
to you!

J Mase III

For Jerome Mason.

Table of Contents

Quick Note: There are multiple ways to read this book. You can read it straight through, so we can both get to know each other a bit. If you want just happy pieces, stick to the Blessings. If you want my story, check out the Rants. If you only want to focus on your grief work, check out the worksheets and anything with grief in the title. If you just want poems, they are simply labeled with their titles. If you want to focus on your art sustainability alone, check out Rant 5 and the Artist Worksheet section.

I think it's my responsibility to warn you.

The story appearing in this book, may not end well. I can't tell you yet, if this is a story with a happy ending or a sad one, or maybe an anti-climactic whimper, but I am committed to us at least trying to find that out together. If you're up for a journey with no certain finish, then I'm here.

Before we get started, you should probably know who I am.

My name is "J Mase III". If that's too long, you can call me "Mase" or "J Mase" for short. If you ever feel like calling me "J", you should promptly put down this book and don't open it back up again. Can we agree on that rule? We can? Are you sure? Great! Cause I am really testy these days.

This story starts in November of 2012 when I picked up and moved from my home in Philly and headed north to New York City. What happened once I got to

New York isn't about the city so much, just a series of unfortunate events, bad jokes and horrible timing on the part of one little transqueer poet, i.e. me. So, within this book, as we figure out this story's potential outcomes, you should expect to hear some poems, rants, and a few things to keep yourself busy just in case your heart may be a little heavy too.

Maybe we can be friends?

My grandmother died a month after I left Philly. I got to be with her the last couple days of her life. There was a snow storm. My aunt was worried I'd get stuck and rushed me out the door. She died a few hours later. My grandmother was a seer. She read playing cards, chicken bones, tea and your weird ass energy if you came through the door the wrong way. I'd like to think I too can see shit. Sometimes, what I see gets stuck on the past, but I'm working on it.

I'd like to imagine that part of my healing from grief, and life, as a Black Trans person is understanding the legacy I am a part of.

Dear Trans Person,

You have a right to heal.

Zone of Rarity

True story
the other day
I dreamt I was cuddling with a human
sized platypus.
I stroked its beak and its tail
I wrapped my arms around it
and it made a sound I did not
recognize
but that sound
felt a lot like joy and calm and loyalty
I hear some call that love
And maybe I didn't know what love
sounded like
until that moment
but that's not surprising to me
because sometimes survivors are like
that
We're used to mistaking chaos for
love

We've been trained to call our very realities
things that they are not
So this clarity in my spirit was new
I woke up all rejuvenated
and wanted to know everything about
the love of my dreams
So I read every encyclopedia entry
every Wikipedia article
Listened to every Ted Talk I came across
about the platypus
but they all described it the same way
Said that it was weird and strange
That it had the bill of a duck
and the tail of a beaver
But how foolish does that sound to the Platypus
that you could be saying it has the tail
of a creature

it's never even shared the same
continent with
It's like
if it has the bill of a Platypus
and the tail of a Platypus
and poison spurs in its feet like a
Platypus
it's probably not a duck
It's like calling a thing a thing it is not
It's like when
colonizers that called themselves
scientists
landed on what was once a Black
continent
we now call Australia
You know when they first saw the
Platypus
they thought it was a joke
They thought that someone was
playing a trick
so they tried to remove the bill from
the face of the Platypus

and subsequently killed a lot of
Platypuses that way
trying to uncover the joke
Turns out the joke was murder
Because they were insistent on calling
a thing a thing it was not
Maybe my gender is a Platypus
Folks always labeling parts of my
body
things that they are not
It's sort of like
when Columbus landed on Española
and Balboa landed in North America
and Hawkins landed in West Africa
and they saw all these Black & Brown
bodies
They saw men and women
and they saw something else that they
thought was a joke
They saw all these people that lay
between

their understandings of gender
Sometimes somehow even beyond
them
Some called us healers
Some called us just purely divine
Now some of us just call it trans for
short
But to them it was a joke, someone
playing a trick
So maybe that's why
they ordered us killed by dogs
Maybe that's why
they burned us alive
Maybe that's why they tried to kill
everyone that ever saw us as holy
Maybe that's the punchline
cause the joke to white supremacy is
always murder
It's like
when they told us they were bringing
us civility

on Black & Brown soil
but what they meant
was that they were bringing us the
transatlantic slave trade
Because they like to call a thing a
thing that it is not
It's sort of like maybe my name is a
Platypus
Cause when I say it
people tell me that that's not what it
should be
When really
my ancestors called for me and I
responded back
And they told me there is nothing
Blacker
than me calling my own name into
existence
But to you maybe it's a joke
And maybe that joke is suppression
Because supremacy always tries to kill
things it doesn't understand

You know I hear abusers do that
sometimes
try to devalue things they don't
understand
and call things things that they are
not
So I may call that gaslighting
They may call it law & order
They make call it civility
They may call it a joke or a trick on
them
a trick on their science
a trick on their biology
a trick on their power
a trick on their legal system
a trick on their supremacy
a trick on their superiority
a trick on their religiosity
But there will always be the Platypus
Even when you laugh behind its back
Even when you deny its power it has
poison in every step it takes

Underwater it senses electrical pulses
to find its food
and the things that it will prey on
It reminds me of myself and the ways
that I sense bullshit
and decide what kinds of energy I will
or will not feed on
even when you think I am a joke
that my body is weird and strange
even when you call me a thing a thing
I am not
Maybe I am not a Platypus
Maybe I am just defiance with venom
in my walk
Maybe it is just my familiar
Maybe I am just familiar with the
ways white supremacy works
Maybe my familiar teaches me
to always call a thing
exactly What it is
and I
call

you

My father died three months after my grandmother. He was the person that taught me that loving a person meant being willing to be transformed by them. He was born in 1943 in Virginia and was raised within the Nation of Islam. I always called him 'Sir'. Not because he required it, it was just the name I gave him. I held his hand every time I saw him til I was 28. I held his hand the last day I saw him too.

He had a stroke. An unpredictable occurrence. He never drank or smoke. He worked out most of his life. His only curse word was "suckers" and he would apologize profusely for using it.

Got a call from his wife the night after, a woman who is Christian in the kind of way only bigots can be. I camped out with her at the hospital for 10 days. It was March. For things to grow come Spring, the soil must be tended to. My hero was planted like a seed into the earth.

I thought my grandmother's death was unbearable at times. She was the second person in my life I watched change like that. From flesh to ghost. From life, to abyss. My father's death changed my entire reality. I didn't really know what death was before that. And years later, ain't no part of me can be the person I was before.

Heartbreak Is

Heartbreak is a gurgling sound
It is the sound of breath leaving the body
It is the third body
you left like that

Heartbreak is the sound your phone
makes
when it's been days since you got
a call
a text
and the one person you want to tell
won't wake up again
It's the sound of being a teenager and
wondering if you have feelings at all
It is being an adult
and wondering if you can stop
feeling so much

It is the way your tears
sound like they are coming from a
demon
one you haven't met before

one that takes over after you've blacked
out on grief
on liquor
on drugs
on whatever was around to comfort you

Heartbreak is holding your dad's hand
for the last time
in a hospital room
knowing he cannot speak
knowing you cannot understand
knowing even if you could talk through
tears
he can't hear you

Heartbreak is knowing every abuser you
have ever had
will always be at more parties
be more extroverted
have more friends
More lovers
and way less insecurities
since they passed down theirs to you

Heartbreak is realizing the most lovable
shiny bits of you
are papier-mâché pieces
of whatever mask
you use
to protect people you love
from the sadness of you
The grey parts
with no silver lining
that fester
in the dark

Heartbreak
is realizing the world
doesn't believe in fairness
and the shit your parents told you
as a child
about good people
and bad people
were just lies
they told you
so you had more
to hold on to
than they did

It is knowing
that this ache
might never go away
That a single name
a word
a syllable or two
can have it all crash down

It is knowing that sanity
is a made up condition
that there isn't always time to heal
if you want to stay alive

Heartbreak is knowing
some days
you struggle to be alive
and wonder
if all this is real tomorrow
what the hell
was the point
Heartbreak is knowing that at some
point
you'll have to just forgive God

they don't know how hard it is to be
human sometimes

It is knowing that no one is coming to
rescue you
from reality
that this is sometimes all there is

Heartbreak is knowing you'll choose to
do this again
because the uncertainty is scarier

Like if you could just hear a voice once
you'd do something different

If you could see something once
you'd stop being afraid

Heartbreak is knowing that you can
always experience
more pain
and it is safer to manage the wounds
you've got

Dear Trans Person,

Your feelings are real, vital & important.

This book stems from my loss of Sir and grandmother and family, but as Trans folks we know there are so many different types of *Grief* that go unrecognized within a cis framework.

For trans people know   *Grief*

There is *Grief*   for the people who will never accept us

There is *Grief*   for our chosen family that we may outlive

There is *Grief*   for those we see in newspapers who look like us

There is *Grief*   for the lies told about our bodies

and *Grief*   that is held within our flesh

For Trans people who know *Grief*, let this be a moment to breathe out all the grief you are carrying. The *Grief* you did/do not deserve. The *Grief* you are a master at forgetting.

B
........R
    ....E
       ....A
         ....T
           ....H
             ....E

Grieving Bill of Rights:

1. You have a right to cry in public places. Your tears will hit new octaves. Feel free to make an opera on every street corner that will have you.

2. Even if you are crazy (which any sane person will be), you have a right not to be around people who make you feel that way.

3. You have a right to stay in bed motionless for at least a week. Turn yourself every few hours to avoid bed sores or stick with the pain just as a reminder that you are alive.

4. God/the Universe/the World/Existence, whichever you want to pick is evil. Trust no one.

5. Accept that whoever you lost, wants to see you do well. So, don't get up every day for yourself if you find your life meaningless. Live long enough in their

honor for you to reach some type of happiness.

Being Black and Trans is a blessing from the Orishas. The problem with the world is that rarely are there places for Black Trans people to be human. When Sir was in the hospital, tubes all which a way, I got a call from my supervisor...she wanted to know when I'd be back at work.

"He's in a coma."

"Yeah, but you already took time off."

"Because my grandmother was dying..."

"I just thought you'd be back by now."

"I'm never going to see him again."

"We all have to make hard decisions."

I hung up.

Six weeks after Sir died, I opened up my horoscope for the day and it said something to the effect of "Your work situation is about to change. Don't worry, it's for the best." Or something like that. Seriously. I promise I'm not bullshitting you, cause I really don't have the energy to do that. So, was it a shock before then? No. I hated my job and I was so stressed that there wasn't a way for me to feel good about doing it. And I wasn't good at it on a happy day, let alone pile of Mase on the floor major onset grief mode season.

On that day my supervisor called me into her office, where her supervisor and an HR rep were all sitting, stone faced. I was given a letter on crisp white paper that made me feel freer than I had in a long time. I read it twice because I left my glasses home again and it was hard to see the 10 point font of capitalism. I asked them if that meant I could leave "right now?!", they were a bit taken back by my pitch. I hugged everyone in that room and left. It was May 1st. 71 degrees in NYC, trees blooming smelling like pastel dreams, and I'll tell you that day was birthed just for me. I think Sir wanted something more from me than me sitting behind a desk.

A Haiku for My Boss:

To my employer
Fuck yo job I'm a poet
I'm goin' back to bed

Dear Trans Person,

You are glittering purple sequins flickering in the daylight, among all these drab grey sidewalks. Sometimes folks glare at you deflecting their insecurities, realizing they have been wasting their life staring at the ground while you have been reflecting possibility.

Grief makes you really weird. Right after Sir died, I was all 'film Noire' sitting in cheap French cafes close to my job eating escargot and crying into wine during happy hour Monday thru Friday (I am so sorry to the wait staff that had to see me do that for a month). Now that I had no job, I got to grieve full time! And for that reason, this book took forEveR to write. It's painful to write about people that you miss, even worse, it's painful to write about feelings of not being wanted.

Why unwanted? The reality is, that many people you care about have no idea what to do when things go truly wrong. Lots of people will tell you how strong you are, or how sorry they are for your loss. The strong thing always gets me, like existing beyond a tragedy makes you a superhero. No cape here. Just still alive. Being alive after a tragedy is to be in constant hurt. Emotionally and physically. Eating takes effort, headaches are constant, and you find pits in your gut you never knew to look for. You may lose weight, you may gain weight. You may lose sleep and hair. Maybe just the will to even get out of bed. So, instead of waiting on everyone to get their shit together, let's imagine the best parts about grieving, shall we?

1. I can clear a line at the grocery store by bursting into tears.
2. I can avoid talking to people I don't like by making them really uncomfortable in 5 seconds or less by saying, something to the effect of, "Yeah, I used to love that before I watched my Dad die, but now..." and just letting my eyes wander out in space.
3. I've lost so many kinds of fluids, I'm pretty sure that I'll never be tricked into doing one of those fucked up cleanse diets.
4. While surviving doesn't make you a superhero, my good friend tells me that crying related dehydration

might give you superpowers!! Watch out now, it's ***Nuclear Radioactive Depresso Boi*!!!** (Or, just some dude with snot in his nose, tears on his jacket and an empty voicemail box, but you know, same thing.)

5. Grief makes my mind SHARP. I might sound like a disheveled mess, but I know if you followed through on what you said or didn't. It gives me the ability to decipher who is honest and who is just talking out of their ass.

Your turn! ***What are some of the gifts of grief?***

_____

_____

_____

_____

_____

_____

Dear Trans Person,

Thank you for calling yourself into existence.

At some point, I realized I needed to make money. I didn't have the energy to go to a job interview and compete for work at another place I hated because I was too miserable to even fake nice. I needed something that allowed me to **feel** a moment of joy. I wanted to be who grief transformed me into. That was a truth teller. That was someone who needed to share. That was someone who couldn't be on a 9-5, because truth be told, that deep grief that suspends your sense of self ain't on no colonizer time. It says show up, when Spirit says you ready. I needed work that respected me as the Black Trans Brilliance I was ordained to be, and for me, that was doing the art I had always been doing on the side, but not respecting. I decided to become a full-time poet.

For a lot of reasons, the arts are one of the few accessible work forms for Black/Brown Trans folks especially because of all the trauma we face. Having control over our autonomy means less chances to have our humanity questioned and disregarded.

Because I know Black/Brown Trans folks will read this, I want to leave you a little something. Having to hustle for rent last minute in NYC on art, taught me a set of skills I want to share. Here is a worksheet for those of you wanting to do art, but needing a framework to get started.

Artist Worksheet or 'So, You Wanna Manifest?!'

Section 1: My art/work is

In this section, be as specific about your themes and who you'd like to see your art. For example, I wouldn't say that my work is just about "transness". I'd say my work is about Blackness, Transness from the Framework of Black Liberation, Decolonizing Faith, Navigating Survivorship, Poetry as a Tool of Cultural Preservation, etc. In terms of location for your audience, think about what types of places your audience might gather.

1. What themes come up in your art?

_____

_____

_____

_____

_____

_____

_____

2.   Who is your ideal audience?

_____

_____

_____

_____

_____

_____

3.   Where might your ideal audience be located?

_____

_____

_____

_____

_____

_____

4.   Skills I possess that are complementary to my art are (youth work, workshops, etc...):

_____
_____
_____
_____
_____
_____
_____

5.   I make time to rehearse/create/fine tune my craft every____:
a.   week
b.   day
c.   month
d.   What is linear time anyway?!?

Section 2: My financials look like

If I'm honest, this section tends to make people the saddest. The point of this section is not to make you sad, but for those of us who come from targeted communities to critically think about the ways we are trained to give work away for free in a society that feeds off our labor. For those reading this that are TQPOC folks, Black/Brown folks in particular, let us remember that we come from a legacy of folks who deserved the resources they needed to survive and not only didn't get them, but were stolen from. I am invested in cooperative economics and resource sharing. I know that when I have what I need, that my family gets some, my friends get some, and more importantly, we all can be clear on what resources exist and what is possible. So, take out a calculator and your calendar and let's do this together!

1. How many gigs did you acquire this year? _____
   a. Last year? _____
   b. How many were unpaid? Did you pay for any?

   _____

2. On average, you made how much per gig? _____
   a. Was that enough to sustain you? (Y/N)
   b. For how long?_____

3. My monthly bills come to about: $_____.

4. My art pays all my bills or close to it (Y/N).

5. How many gigs would I need to pay my monthly expenses based on my current rate(s)?

   _____

6. I supplement my art income by working _____ additional hours per week.

Section 3: My emergency prep looks like

In this section, take time to think about what your model of pricing would need to look like to *thrive*, not just to barely survive come rent day. Are there folks that rely on you for care? Do you have a disability which makes travel difficult on your body? Think about a pricing and outreach model in which you are shooting to make about 2x as much as you would actually need. Why? Cause things happen! Snow, illness, missed planes; prep like you know the world is mad random. This should also get you thinking about other factors that may need to go into your pricing model.

1. I have money set aside for emergencies if a gig falls through. (Y/N)

    a. If yes, how much?

    _____

2. I have/plan on having children and have access to child care while I am working. (Y/N)

    a. My childcare costs

    _____

3. I have health care. (Y/N)

4. I need to travel with an additional person for health reasons. (Y/N)

5. I have at least one adult in my life that relies solely on my income for care. (Y/N)

    a. I have access to an additional care taker when I am working.

Section 4: My outreach looks like

In this last section, think intentionally about your outreach plan. This is where most folks get tripped up. You can have the most amazing art in the world, but if nobody knows about it, they can't support you. Most artists will lose steam because they sent out one email to two venues five years ago and no one responded. In reality, when you are doing outreach, expect that if these are folks that do not know you, it is normal that only 10% will get back to you the first time. That can seem daunting, but I promise, if you take your outreach seriously, you can put your brilliant work in front of enough folks to get the support you need to make your work sustainable. Make a database of folks and venues to reach out to. Don't take no's or silence personally. It is usually not about you. It tends to be about the fact that the person on the receiving end also has 500 other emails to respond to. That doesn't make you any less brilliant.

1. I reached out to _____ venues/organizations/clients this year.

2. My goal this year is to reach out to _____ venues/organizations/clients.

3. I feel comfortable reaching out to venues/orgs/clients on my own (Y/N).

4. My 30 second elevator pitch about my art/work is (use your answers to section 1 to help you complete this):

_____

_____

_____

_____

_____

_____

_____

_____

_____

_____

_____

_____

_____

_____

_____

_____

_____

_____

_____

_____

_____

_____

_____

_____

5. I use a website and/or social media to advertise my work. (Y/N)

6. ***I actually tell people*** about my website/social media advertising my work. (Y/N)

Okay, now that we've talked about the highs and lows of work during grief...let's talk about the even less sexy topic of dating while being a ball of mess. Dating while you are grieving means you don't always have the best filter. I mean, you kind of feel like a dumpster fire, so what then is the light off a few red flags? Ya know what I mean?

I dated a former minister for a bit. He was also Black & Trans. My upbringing was coming from a Christian and Muslim home, and as an adult, I'd turned into quite the theology nerd. For me, being Black & Trans means to be a holder of Spirit. I loved having someone to talk to about scripture theory and how it relates to trans liberation (Some of y'all just rolled your eyes, I get it). It was everything I thought I needed until it wasn't. I thought I wanted someone who paid me a lot of attention and called first. Someone who was spiritual. What I got was obsessive, a bit of stalking and a lot of PTSD wrapped in internalized anti-trans and anti-gay theology. Even more, I got to witness firsthand how many view their religious practice as a passive thing. So, when I needed help and reached out to clergy who knew all the buzzwords about radical inclusion, they knew nothing about actually supporting folks dealing with violence. I learned to ask better questions about relationships and faith.

Bad Theology: Or a Black Trans Man Attempts Salvation

Is your God a white supremacist?
Do you run your fingers through Jesus's
long silky hair?
Do you hang a photo of a blue eyed deity
on your wall
And wonder if you've ever summoned a
demon?

There was something
about the way he grabbed me in the
middle of the night
like touch was urgent
like maybe he conjured something
he couldn't put back
and this embrace was a spell
to ward off a beast
that haunted him since childhood
Our bed was infested with djinn
and poltergeists
that sometimes slipped

between the cracks in our fingers
and possessed the space
between our bodies
and these sheets
that were churned
from the devil's manifesto

He prayed to Jesus everyday
bright eyed
bushy tailed
pasty ass
Jesus
Rescue us
kindly negroes
from evil

The Devil's hour is somewhere between
3am
and 4

The way he'd jolt awake
you'd think something
was pulling from inside his skin
something nasty

something that wasn't alive anymore
something burning
something ancient and sharp

He'd stare at me through
the space between
these breaks
in our realities
and his fists would be hungry
like they needed
to be fed by something
a table
a lamp
a chair
the wood of this wall
and sometimes
a break in my skin
This thing
needed blood
So here am I
an offering

This creature
craved it

but it was never enough
It colonized our apartment
like a spanish conquistador
like manifest destiny
like when you pray to Gods
that aren't yours
you will only manifest
creatures
that know nothing
of the holiness of
your birth

Is your God a violent God?
Does it keep you up in the middle of the
night
Does it excuse away its indiscretions
at all hours
and try to make peace with you in
daylight
Does your God pray with you?
Does it acknowledge the stretch marks
from your pain
Or does it get off on them

Pastor
What type of ire must I have truly
inspired
to get all that grief
Is your God one that thrives off
destruction
Is he always like this?
Is your God always like this?

Pastor
This God that has escaped
in these walls
of this Church
I think it wants something from me
It wants my ancestors' bones
It wants me weak
It wants me believing
that there ain't no rescue
coming for me

Pastor
Did it make me out of love?
Did it make me in its image?
If your God is out to kill me

does that mean it's trying to crack me
open
to get closer
to my soul

Pastor
Tell whoever you've been praying to
this is my body
It has been broken from what your
followers
have done to me
This blood has been spilled
in Remembrance of you

Pastor
where
is
my
God?

I have lost them
I have lost them
I have lost them

Bonus Worksheet for Sad Faces Tryna Recover/Rediscover Their Humanity

1. What has grief taught you about yourself?

_____

_____

_____

_____

_____

_____

_____

_____

2. What would the person you are grieving say about you? What parts of that would you like to embody, and what would you like to throw away?

_____

_____

_____

_____

_____

_____

_____

_____

_____
_____

3. What do you need in this moment, but haven't gotten or been able to ask for?

_____
_____
_____
_____
_____
_____
_____
_____
_____

4. What movie character are you right now?

_____
_____
_____
_____
_____
_____

_____

_____

5. Name someone that wouldn't judge you for how you are feeling.

_____

_____

_____

_____

_____

_____

6. Name a person, or place you are committed to going to get some support.

_____

_____

_____

_____

_____

7. Name three things you want to accomplish in the next year.

_____

_____

_____

_____

Draw a portrait of the person, entity, tool, creature or spirit that is helping you protect your heart these days:

So, now what? Well, I have my dream job. I am hella single (and okay with it). I have gained and lost many friends. I am not proud of all the things I did and said when I was grieving. The world stops moving. Your brain malfunctions and sputters on the floor. There were times I yelled and screamed and cried and some of the things I meant. Some things I meant, but wish I had a softer way to say them. I was just sad and uncaring.

Grief is a strange thing that changes the longer you outlive it. It makes me want to talk about my Dad/Sir non-stop. So, I warned you at the beginning, that this short book might not have an ending, that it is rambly...Well, life doesn't have closed endings. Because you're here with me this long, I want to share some poems that are inspired by Sir. The ones where he taught me to demand respect. The ones where he was a dad that didn't always want to be. Our relationship wasn't perfect. He was my breakfast buddy on Saturday mornings. He was the person that taught me manhood and faith. I saved every voicemail he ever left me. And, because I can't give you those, these poems will have to do.

April Fools

Dear N,
As per your request
I tried to fit my dad into a poem last
night
and I think it killed him
See my 8 ½ x 11 inch page is not big
enough to fit his arms and legs inside
this ride
So I had to leave parts of him along the
highway
and hope the soft pieces would land
somewhere delicate along my heart
I used to write epic novels
So he lived there for 300 years amongst
the legends
but once I started slamming
his heartbeat became dependent upon
my cadences
and 3 minutes wasn't enough time for
him
to find the rhythm of his breath again
I almost became afraid to lay my lips
upon his name
Because the trauma of him becoming
reanimated left him feeling cold

Like the tip of my pen couldn't fully resuscitate him
and this new pain was getting old
plus I've had to share him with a third wife and an audience
which has left me with only a line here or there to give sporadic cpr
And every time he looks at me
I can tell he won't come back the same because
he refuses sleep anymore
He just keeps replaying in my mind
like these arbitrary timers
are just wasting more and more of his precious time
I tried to stitch him up with metaphor
but the ink would bleed right through
So I tried to immortalize him akin to Nietzsche
but social theorists be not amused
I went back into my childhood to rebuild him with Dr. Seuss
but now he was labeled absentee and deserters get no fuel
So I held him together with pieces of my ribs
spitting rhymes into the night

Hoping the commitment of my
diaphragm
might bring him permanently back to
life
And this could all just be a nightmare
that I might soon forget
But the promise of a good poem is while
there's microphone
no one has to die just yet
So, April fools
she says
Your dad isn't really dead
He's just lost in a poem
tucked away in a notepad
you misplaced in your desk somewhere
If you stay up tonight
all night
I'm sure you'll find it
Just
move around the madness
Throw away the junk and
he'll be standing there
You'll see
Just beyond the darkness of these chairs
and the blankness of this
white page
He is the beginning of you

afterall
and lives every time you speak his name
is what they tell you
like you're a child waiting on Santa
Believe in the power of your fucking
poems
and maybe it will snow
But that's not what you wanted
I wanted him to be real again
Is this poem really going to do that
But you'll compress him
into three minutes
1-8-0 seconds
But after the applause
what are you to do with the silence
when clearly your spell has brought you
no rewards
So if I should die
before I wake
do not resuscitate
do not resuscitate
do not resuscitate *me*
Let me die in peace
And do not try to stir my sleeping spirit
up
by trying to fit me
into one of your tiny

fucking
3 minute
poems

This poem is for one of the final stages of grief, learning to deal with arguments you never had when they were alive, because you loved them. It appears in the theatrical production, **Black Bois**.

The Seventh:

And what are you to do
with ghosts
Do you pay them attention
Do you honor them
Do you become disgusted
with yourself for wanting to fight them
It was 5 years
after the fact
that I thought to myself
Hey
maybe the guy
who cheated on you
3 times
wasn't such a nice guy
maybe he was just a guy
who couldn't keep it in his pants

Maybe he was a guy
who thought his dick
was more important than honesty
maybe he just thought you were
too stupid
to say anything
I mean you never did
and you knew
and you wonder
where on Earth did you learn this loyalty
for men
who refuse your boundaries
For men that would rather
string you along
and suddenly you find yourself arguing
with ghosts
named after your father
Trying to have conversations
that should have happened
when that man was still alive
So he could grow into a man
that would have taught you self respect
and holding loyalty
for people

who see you as someone
Sacred

This Heart

This heart
is mine
mine to give
mine to receive
mine to love
whoever is
worthy

And let me prepare myself
Let me allow my heart to break open
with a possibility of abundance
May my heart
Flow
like rain
drowning out
my doubts
May they be abandoned
in the wilderness
and left to rot
May they serve as the compost
to nurture what I have left to grow
For

many a dream has died within me
but left their seeds upon my flesh
May they come into fruition again
with stronger sense
Of purpose
Of skill
Of finding light
where shadow was prevalent
May these wounds heal

Dear Trans Person,

Thank you for sharing yourself with this greedy world.

Photo of Sir at
diner by
J Mase III

Acknowledgements:

Thank you to Dane, Elle, Andy, Jenn, Mother Mason, David, Déjà, Ajamu, Amelia, Yalini, and everyone else that made this book possible.

And most of all, thank you to Mr. Mason for your wisdom, love and friendship.

About the Author

J Mase III is a Black/trans/queer poet &  educator based in Seattle by way of Philly. As an educator, Mase has worked with thousands of community members in the US, UK, and Canada on LGBTQIA+ rights and racial justice in spaces such as K-12 schools, universities, faith communities and restricted care facilities. He is founder of awQward, the first trans and queer people of color specific talent agency.

His work has been featured on MSNBC, Essence Live, Everyday Feminism, Black Girl Dangerous, the New York Times, Buzzfeed, the Root, theGrio, Teen Vogue, TEDx and more.

His current projects include being the head writer of the theatrical production, ***Black Bois*** and being co-editor of the ***#BlackTransPrayerBook***.

When he is not working, he is obsessed with his dog, Nikki G who also aspires to be a poet one day.

Find him on Instagram (@jmaseiii) and www.jmaseiii.com!